Best Wishes

Roy H. Vickers

Oct 1980

# The Elders Are Watching

# The Elders Are Watching

## Dave Bouchard
Text

## Roy Henry Vickers
Images

# Roy Henry Vickers

Roy Vickers is a phenomenon. His unique and dramatic artistic style – contemporary designs which have evolved from his earlier traditional Northwest Coast Indian art, has won him a passionate following. It is not unusual for his original paintings and the accompanying limited edition of fifty serigraphs to be purchased prior to their conception.

His powerful images are a composition of simplicity, bold lines and either stunning or subdued colours. They invite the audience to interpret subtleties and nuances. These creations are a direct result of Vickers' commitment to his heritage and his environment – especially the West Coast of British Columbia. To study his work is to almost experience this impressive part of the world and its history.

Roy Vickers is an outdoorsman. To say that he is an ardent fisherman is an understatement; he is fanatical about this pursuit. His escapades are constantly being captured in his paintings.

He is a man of considerable talents. In addition to being a painter and a sportfisherman, Roy is a carver, a designer of jewellery and furniture, and a musician. His ability as a writer is documented in the very readable text in his first book, *Solstice, The Art of Roy Henry Vickers*.

From his home base in Tofino, British Columbia and his incredible longhouse – Eagle Aerie Gallery, Roy Vickers is making an impact on Canadian art. Patrons of his work come not only from across the country and throughout North America, but from Europe and the Far East as well.

# Thoughts

Revival, culture, heritage, environment. These are key words for this last decade of the century.

We now find ourselves fighting a battle to turn a tide of destruction that has been rising for too many years and threatens to drown the family unit, our social structure and our environment. We have been overly self-indulgent for much too long, and it is time for change.

Change comes from understanding ourselves – our weaknesses, our strengths. That understanding can be fostered from knowledge of our past, our cultural heritage and our environment. This priceless wisdom is available from our elders, who like us, received it from their ancestors.

We all have elders, ancestors and a cultural heritage. Once we know our past, we have taken a step in understanding ourselves, and we will then be able to strengthen our truths, bringing about changes for the better.

Such changes can affect our many relationships – intimate ones, social and professional ones, and the one we have with our environment. These actions will help us to turn the tide, letting it wash over the land, healing those wrongs we have had a part in creating.

Roy Henry Vickers

# Dave Bouchard

Dave Bouchard is a writer and a teller of stories. Nothing gives him more pleasure than to share that which he has written and the stories of favourite authors such as Byrd Baylor, Roald Dahl and Orin Cochrane.

Dave is an administrator in the British Columbia public schools system. He was born and raised on the prairies. After seventeen years of teaching in Regina and three in Lahr, West Germany, Dave, his wife Mary and their two sons Adrien and Etienne, made the move as so many before them had done, from the prairies to beautiful British Columbia.

It was through his love for art that Dave began writing. He had been a collector of art for years and thought it a real shame that students were not being exposed to more wonderful art, the kind that was all around them and appreciated by adults. This belief initiated the idea for his first book, *White Tails Don't Live In The City*. The children's book was illustrated by Ken Lonechild, a Cree native from the White Bear Reserve in southern Saskatchewan.

"I was first exposed to the work of Roy Henry Vickers shortly after our family's arrival in Vancouver. I immediately recognized his style as a form of art that would be easily accepted by youth as well as adults. I was struck by Roy's perception of the world. The inspiration for writing *The Elders Are Watching* came quickly and clearly. My eventual meeting of Roy and his family in his incredibly wonderful world of Clayquot Sound around Tofino was equally gratifying."

Both Roy and Dave share similar dreams for their children. Through *The Elders Are Watching*, it is hoped that others will come to share these dreams, and together work toward correcting some of the mistakes of the past.

Dave and his family now live in Deep Cove, North Vancouver. He is currently working with artist, Charles Van Sandwyck to create another unique children's book. Also upcoming is a further collaboration with Ken Lonechild entitled, *Friends, If You're Not From The Prairie*. A sequel to *White Tails…* is also planned.

# Whispers

The boy looked much the same as the other kids in his class. New faces arrived almost daily from far away places, so it wasn't his appearance that made him different.

He had always tried his hardest, but try as he might, somehow he didn't seem to be able to get excited about the same things his classmates did. This year was no different.

And so, as in years gone by, his mother would please him greatly by taking him out of school for a time. Again she was sending him off to live with his grandfather, his 'Ya-A' – to listen, to think and to learn.

'Ya-A' would reintroduce him to the Wind, the Tree and the Earth. 'Ya-A' would speak of responsibilities and of rights. 'Ya-A' would fascinate him with legends of the eagle, the whale, the raven and the wolf.

Of all the tales his grandfather told, none captured his heart more than the stories of the Old Ones – the Elders. And as the stories slowly became part of him, by the seashore in the clear red sky of early evening, he began to see them.

They appeared as images suspended in the air, up toward the sun. Their lips were still, yet he heard them speak. Their message, like the words of his 'Ya-A', was clear and true, a message gone too long without being passed to other hearts.

He and his 'Ya-A' would share the words of the Elders often with all those who cared to listen – with all those who cared at all.

*Dave Bouchard*

Dave Bouchard

They told me to tell you they believed you
When you said you would take a stand.
They thought that you knew the ways of nature.
They thought you respected the land.

*Look to the Mountain*

Look To The Mountain

1/50

They want you to know that they trusted you
With the earth, the water, the air,
With the eagle, the hawk and the raven,
The salmon, the whale and the bear.

*Eagle's Moon*

You promised you'd care for the cedar and fir,
The mountains, the sea and the sky.
To the Elders these things are the essence of life.
Without them a people will die.

*Old Town*

*They told me to tell you the time has come.*
*They want you to know how they feel.*
*So listen carefully, look toward the sun.*
*The Elders are watching.*

*A Meeting of Chiefs*

A MEETING OF CHIEFS

They wonder about risking the salted waters,
The ebb and flow of running tide.
You seem to be making mistakes almost daily.
They're angry, they're hurting, they cry.

*Chinook*

1/50                    Chinook

The only foe the huge forest fears
Is man, not fire, nor pest.
There are but a few who've come to know
To appreciate nature's best.

*Meares Island*

They watch as you dig the ore from the ground.
You've gone much too deep in the earth.
The pits and scars are not part of the dream
For their home, for the place of their birth.

*Chief's Dream*

*They told me to tell you the time has come.*
*They want you to know how they feel.*
*So listen carefully, look toward the sun.*
*The Elders are watching.*

*Siwash Rock*

They say you hunt for the thrill of the kill.
First the buffalo, now the bear.
And that you know just how few there are left,
And yet you don't seem to care.

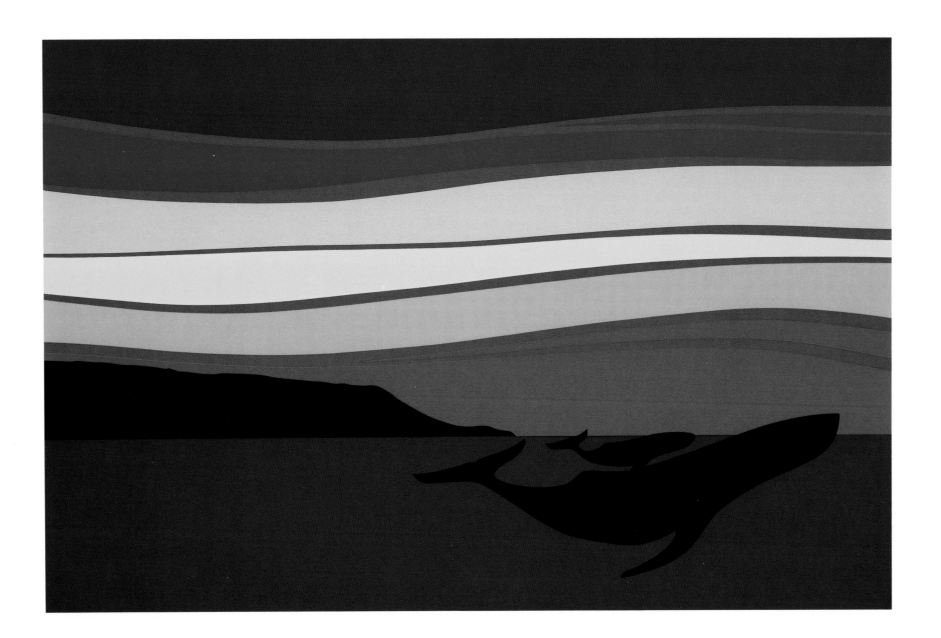

They have no problem with fishing for sport.
There are lots of fish in the sea.
It is for the few who will waste a catch,
For you, they are speaking through me.

*Steelhead*

You said you needed the tree for its pulp,
You'd take but a few, you're aware
Of the home of the deer, the wolf, the fox,
Yet so much of their land now stands bare.

*Cedar Snags*

*They told me to tell you the time has come.*
*They want you to know how they feel.*
*So listen carefully, look toward the sun.*
*The Elders are watching.*

*Where is Kitkatla?*

They're starting to question the things that you said
About bringing so much to their land.
You promised you'd care for their daughters and sons,
That you'd walk with them hand in hand.

A/P II/X          Dreams of the Past

But with every new moon you seem to be
More concerned with your wealth than the few
Women and children, their bloodline, their heartbeat,
Who are now so dependent on you.

VISIONS OF THE FUTURE

You are offering to give back bits and pieces
Of the land they know to be theirs.
Don't think they're not grateful, it's just hard to say so
When wondering just how much you care.

*Ninstints*

1/50

NINSTINTS

*They told me to tell you the time has come.*
*They want you to know how they feel.*
*So listen carefully, look toward the sun.*
*The Elders are watching.*

*Carmanah*

11/50                    CARMANAH                    Roy H. Vicke
                                                     5/12/87

Now friend be clear and understand
Not everything's dark and glum.
They are seeing some things that are making them smile,
And that's part of the reason I've come.

*Going to the Potlatch*

Going to the Potlatch

The colour green has come back to the land.
It's for people who feel like me.
For people who treasure what nature gives,
For those who help others to see.

*Guardian of the Pass*

And there are those whose actions show.
They see the way things could be.
They do what they can, give all that they have
Just to save one ancient tree.

*They told me to tell you the time has come.*
*They want you to know how they feel.*
*So listen carefully, look toward the sun.*
*The Elders are watching.*

Of all of the things that you've done so well,
The things they are growing to love,
It's the sight of your home, the town that you've built.
They can see it from far up above.

*Vancouver*

Like the sun when it shines, like the full moon at night,
Like a hundred totems tall,
It has brightened their sky and that's partially why
They've sent me to you with their call.

Now I've said all the things that I told them I would.
I hope I am doing my share.
If the beauty around us is to live through this day
We'd better start watching – and care.

*They told me to tell you the time is now.*
*They want you to know how they feel.*
*So listen carefully, look toward the sun.*
*The Elders are watching.*

CANADIAN CATALOGUING IN PUBLICATION DATA

Bouchard, Dave, 1952-
    The elders are watching
    A poem.

    ISBN 0-9693485-3-3

1. Man – Influence on nature – Poetry.
2. Indians of North America – Poetry. I.
Vickers, Roy Henry, 1946-    II. Title.
PS8553.093E4 1990    C811'.54    C90-091299-5
PR9199.3.B68E4 1990


Designers: Roy Henry Vickers & Ken Budd
Editor: Ken Budd
Printing: Hemlock Printers Ltd.
            Vancouver, B.C.


Produced by:
Ken Budd, Executive Producer

Summer Wild
PRODUCTIONS

#2202 – 1275 Pacific Street
Vancouver, B.C. V6E 1T6
Phone (604) 681-0015


Published by:
EAGLE DANCER ENTERPRISES LTD.
P.O. Box 527, Tofino, B.C., Canada V0R 2Z0
Phone (604) 725-3235    Fax: (604) 725-4466